HOPE
In the Hands of Fatima

PHOTOGRAPHY & WORDS BY CHRISTINE SPRING

Beatnik

Beatnik Publishing

PO Box 8276, Symonds Street, Auckland 1150, New Zealand.
www.beatnikpublishing.com

First published in 2016
by Beatnik Publishing in association with Christine Spring.

www.christinespring.com

Text: copyright © Christine Spring 2016
Photography: copyright © Christine Spring in association with UNICEF NZ 2016
Design and Typesetting: copyright © Beatnik Design Limited 2016

This book is copyright. Apart from any fair dealing for the purposes of private study, research or review, as permitted under the Copyright Act, no part may be reproduced by any process without the permission of the publishers.

This visit to Lebanon included:
UNICEF NZ Executive Director, Vivien Maidaborn
UNICEF NZ Good Will Ambassador, Sonny Bill Williams
UNICEF NZ Sports Manager, Andre Whittaker
UNICEF Communication Specialist, Salam Abdulmunem
UNICEF Communications Consultant, Hiba Shaaban
TV 3 Journalist, Mike McRoberts
TV 3 Cameraman, Nick Zieltjes
Photographer, Christine Spring
Sonny Bill's Manager, Khoder Nasser
Printed and bound in China.

ISBN 978-0-9941205-4-0

For Fatima,

To honour her and her desire for hope for her family and fellow refugees.

You are not forgotten.

A VISIT

On December 7 and 8 2015, Sonny Bill Williams accompanied the UNICEF NZ Executive Director, Vivien Maidaborn and TV3 journalist Mike McRoberts on a visit to Syrian refugee informal settlements in the Bekaa Valley, Lebanon. The objective of their visit was to use television and social media coverage to raise awareness of the refugees, their desperation and their need for help.

The visit resulted in two 4-minute news stories, a flurry of Facebook posts and numerous news articles, but these were delivered around Christmas time and, in the midst of the festivities, seemingly swiftly put aside and forgotten.

Yet the photographs that were taken of the refugees tell a compelling and very different story to that which we often hear and see in the news. The images speak of children impacted by the crisis in their homeland – Syria. The images provide a glimpse of the seemingly hopeless future that they now face. The photos also document the projects provided by UNICEF and their NGO partners.

These children are in need of protection and just want to be able to get an education, and have hope for a future.

They are just like our children, just kids – who through no fault of their own have experienced trauma, been displaced, and live with great uncertainty.

The message that these children hold in their faces is actually a universal message – all children, irrespective of nationality and the circumstance of their situation, deserve the right to be cared for, be protected, and receive an education. They deserve to have HOPE for a happy life.

Throughout 2015, images of deadly sea crossings to Europe focused international attention on Syria's refugee crisis. But the vast majority of those fleeing Syria's civil war, including the most vulnerable, are not travelling to Europe. They are remaining in the Middle East, living marginal existences with uncertain futures.

The impact of the Syria conflict continues to shape UNICEF's efforts in Lebanon. By October 2015, the number of Syrian refugees in Lebanon had surpassed 1.1 million, equivalent to an additional 25% of Lebanon's pre-crisis population. Lebanon now hosts more refugees

The single location enables UNICEF to erect tents and focus on four key areas of assistance: Health, yOuth, Protection and Education, aka H.O.P.E.

per capita than any other country in the world. Some 53% of the refugees are children. The crisis has meant that, in addition to the Syrian refugees, there are also greater numbers of poor and marginalised Lebanese and Palestinian refugee children at risk of exclusion and exploitation. The reality is that there are now 3 million refugees and vulnerable Lebanese in Lebanon, equating to roughly 55% of the country's total population.

The visit by UNICEF NZ was focused on the Saadnayel and Oumarieh informal settlements, where a "convergence of services" model is operated by UNICEF and its NGO partner Beyond Association. The child-friendly space is in effect a large fenced area, surrounded by the informal refugee settlements. The single location enables UNICEF to erect tents and focus on four key areas of assistance: Health, yOuth, Protection and Education, aka H.O.P.E. With this focus they offer a range of services and activities including: psychological support through theatre and handicraft activities; play and learning activities; and mobile medical services.

It is here that the UNICEF NZ team members each had the opportunity to talk and connect with refugees. Accompanied by a cameraman and a photographer, the New Zealanders were warmly welcomed with humble gratitude. The refugees were seemingly thankful that people cared enough to visit and hopeful that, when the visit was over and the cameras put away, they would not be forgotten.

A SAFE SPACE

Entering the gates of the fenced child-friendly space, you are not sure what to expect, or how the spirits of the refugees will be. We had been warned that it would be cold, with winter and snow on its way, but on this day the sun shone and children played outside. At first glance, you perhaps wonder what all the fuss is about and think "do these smiling laughing children really need our help?"

Then you realise that without the intervention of UNICEF and Beyond Association, these children would have no friendly space to go to, no single place that would provide care for their health, education and mental wellbeing. Within this fenced space, the children know they are safe and that they are free to just be kids.

First impressions…

The psychosocial support activities are a core component of the work undertaken by UNICEF. Through recreational activities the refugee children are guided to re-embrace play and learning.

These children have seen and experienced all manner of hardship, atrocity, violence and deprivation, and for many of them the mental and emotional trauma is significant. By providing them with a safe environment to visit daily, and by enabling the children to embrace music, theatre, animation and handicrafts, UNICEF hopes that they can begin to process their experiences and find a way to grow their own hope for the future. It was, at first, strange to see kids running around in Santa Claus costumes – not what we had expected to encounter at all – but they were just practising for their Christmas pantomime!

A ball and a fun game provide universal joy.

Outside of the UNICEF children's space, the reality of the refugees' hardship is abundantly clear. There is little distinction between men's and women's work. In this environment, you do what you are allowed to and what you must – even if it means transporting cast iron on your head. With a conflict that is now five years old, these once-middle-class Syrians have no savings left to fall back on, nor government benefit to receive. It is up to them to find a way to clothe and feed themselves and their families. Seeing this woman walking by had us wondering how she found the strength for a load that few would have the fortitude and ability to carry.

The reality of informal settlements… rubbish, sewage and poor hygiene are constant concerns.

When fortunate, women can find menial work in the fields.

When there is no work to do, there is sisterhood and strength to be gained… even among a field of litter.

Despite the surrounds and circumstances, parents still discipline…

…and children are cared for by families just doing their best.

The Saadnayel informal settlement is found in the Zahle area of the Bekaa Valley, just an hour's drive over the hill from metropolitan Beirut and 30 minutes from the Syrian border. Dwellings are sporadically located on land that the refugees must rent for about US$250 a month. The location of the settlement can take you by surprise. One minute you are driving on a highway beside shops and apartments, then with a couple of turns and a distance of less than 500m you have arrived. From their homes, the refugees see a vista of housing that they just cannot afford to rent. As winter swiftly approaches, heating becomes a primary concern - there is limited wood, but abundant plastic rubbish. This 'fuel' warms for a moment, emits a toxic stench and is a source of respiratory illness.

In winter, the child-friendly spaces also provide a warm haven for the children – reducing the need for fuel at home.

HEALTH

Health and nutrition programmes are one of the four cornerstones of UNICEF's response to the refugee crisis in Lebanon. Through the mobile medical units, refugees are able to benefit from free, quality, primary health care and children under 5 years old can be included in immunisation programmes for measles, mumps, rubella, and polio. In addition, there is a focus on tetanus vaccination for women of child-bearing age. The aim of the medical intervention is to reduce mortality and ensure that the endemic diseases of tetanus and tuberculosis are kept controlled. Each medical team can reach 80 people a day and costs UNICEF just US$8 per patient to run. UNICEF supports 21 teams across Lebanon.

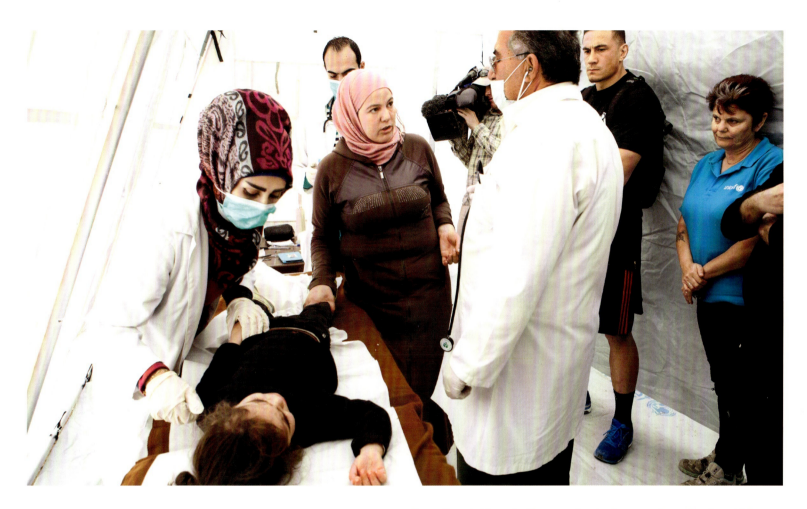

No matter what her situation, a mother is always anxious when her child needs to go to hospital, especially when she cannot afford the treatment nor rely on a public health system.

This young girl was 'lucky' – the NGO agreed to cover the costs.

On the day UNICEF NZ visited, there was a focus on polio immunisation and the young patients were very nervous!

Provision of spectacles is rare…

…blindness providing another layer of struggle for a refugee child.

There are 430 children from five surrounding informal settlements that attend activities at the child-friendly site that UNICEF NZ visited – 38 of these children are orphans and 7 have disabilities, including several with blindness. Watching the children is interesting. When they are engaged in activities, distracted, they seem to be able to put aside their trauma for a few moments and smile. When their minds are busy playing sport or a musical instrument, drawing, writing, or making handicrafts, they seem to escape the reality of their daily life. But then in moments of inactivity their little faces revert to reflecting the magnitude of their situation. In repose, these children seem to emit an indescribable sadness.

Without distracting activities, home life sometimes holds little joy.

The older children are encouraged to write down their stories.

Finding the courage and voice to share the written words can be a struggle.

Yet these children show extraordinary respect, consideration and patience for each other as they find the strength to speak their truth.

With safety and support in numbers, the children sometimes find it easier to write a song and sing together. Their songs reflect the things that are important to them – "We are human too and deserve a right to education". They sung with heartfelt emotion and it was not hard to be affected by the energy and passion of their words and actions. With translation provided, we were able to appreciate the words of these children as they sung songs for peace and the right to be protected. They may be refugees, but they are first and foremost children, young souls facing a difficult and uncertain life.

The sincerity of the children's words and expressions reinforced that this is a place that cares for children's physical, mental and emotional health. It is a place where they can learn coping mechanisms to process the impact of the trauma they have experienced.

For the younger children, a big part of healing comes when they understand that they are not alone and have not been abandoned – a hug from your big brother is often the perfect dose of medicine to wipe away tears and reinforce a sense of safety.

The child-safe space is also a place to help young girls realise that their long-term mental health and wellbeing will be dependent on their ability to set boundaries and demand their right to be protected.

YOUTH

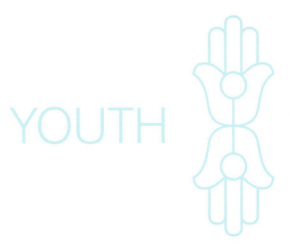

There are approximately one million youths (15-24 year olds) in Lebanon of which an estimated 520,000 are considered vulnerable. Of these, there are close to 100,000 Syrian refugees of secondary school age. In the 2015 school year, only 6% of them were enrolled in formal education in Lebanon. With a focus on equity for all vulnerable youth (poor Lebanese, Palestinian and Syrian refugees), UNICEF and its partners are providing access to basic literacy and numeracy, skills training, and employability training. There is also a focus on life skills: education in conflict management, risky behaviour prevention, and crisis-coping mechanisms.

All children and youth deserve the right to protection and education...

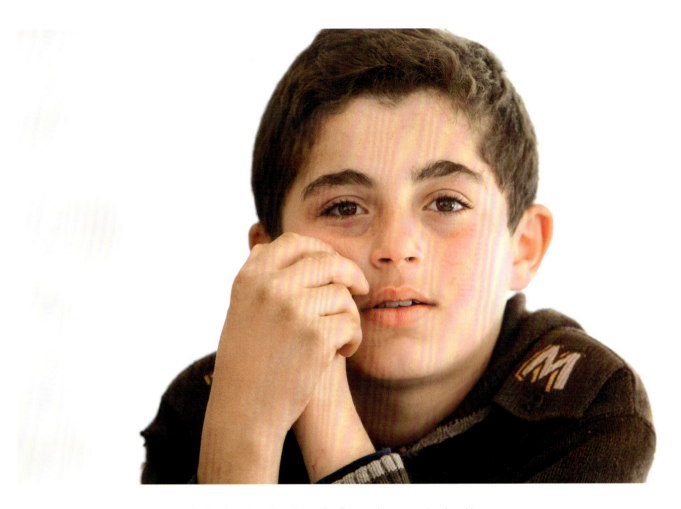

...and a place to feel safe, where they have the time and space to heal and learn.

Because refugees are not officially recognised, men are not able to work and often the only way rent and basic costs can be met is through child labour. Young boys receive $15 per day to help support their families. The burden of responsibility at such a young age is sobering…

…but despite the hardships faced, families are still capable of laughter and can display a very real sense of the love and genuine affection that binds them together. They are survivors and their experiences seem to have heightened a deep desire to protect and care for each other – to the best of their ability.

UNICEF runs life skills classes to help provide the young men with coping mechanisms to deal with their unique financial and emotional pressures.

Once a boy becomes a teenager, there are fewer ways for him to earn money locally and there can then be significant pressure to accept the US$500 a month that rebel recruiters offer for returning to Syria, to fight.

The situation is equally fragile for teenage girls.

Classes for young women focus on 'How to say "no" to early marriage'.

In the face of multiple pressures, including (ironically) a desire to protect their daughters: refugees have an ever-growing tendency to marry girls at 12 or 13 years of age – an action that often strips away their daughters' basic rights and education opportunities.

UNICEF data are indicating that 25% of Syrian girls in Lebanon are forced into marriage before the age of 16. The same context that is increasing male violence against women and leading to boy soldiers is causing an increase in child marriage.

Children of 13 years old should not be brides; girls and women – no matter what age – should not be victims of violence.

UNICEF's youth interventions are focused on education, life skills and learning opportunities.

They hope to build youths' knowledge, skills and resilience so they can become social agents of change in their communities. Where necessary, UNICEF will also target intervention for high-risk youth who are victims of violence, engaged in armed conflict, or engaged in the worst forms of child labour.

The youth focus is important. UNICEF hopes to create opportunities and alternative choices – so that boys don't need to return to Syria to earn a livelihood by fighting and girls don't have to become child brides.

Through its various programmes, UNICEF hopes to help the children develop the skills and knowledge that they need to be able to assert their basic human rights…

…and gain the strength and self-belief to know that they have the capacity and right to create a future for themselves devoid of violence.

PROTECTION

When a child has experienced the trauma of war and been displaced from their homeland, their vulnerability is magnified.

The concern for a child in this situation is not just caused by the immediate and present danger. UNICEF has gathered significant evidence that violence, exploitation and abuse can affect a child's physical and mental health in the short and longer term, impairing their ability to learn and socialise, and impacting on their transition to adulthood with adverse consequences later in life.

This is why it is so important that a child in such a situation is protected, and it is why protection is one of the four cornerstones of UNICEF's work in Lebanon.

Beside his mother a child is secure...

…in her arms he is safe.

Women babysit so girls can attend life skills classes.

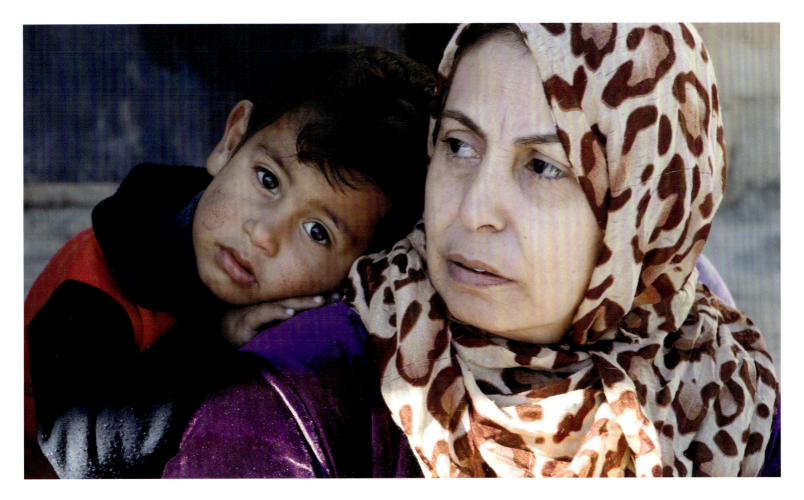
A mother's shoulders provide shelter from a harsh reality.

Without protection, there is little hope of staying out of harm's way.

Spending time in UNICEF's child-friendly spaces and attending life skills and education classes, benefits both mother and child, as the mother gains the knowledge and confidence to nurture and protect.

A mother suffers when she realises that in her eagerness to safeguard her daughter she supported an early marriage that led to her daughter becoming the victim of abuse and violence.

The more education a girl and her mother have, the more they will both learn to speak up and the more likely it will be that the girl can be protected from an early marriage.

Without protection...

...there is little hope of a safe and happy future.

Without protection…

...there is little hope of a peaceful life.

There are many refugees that are simply the proud parents of a newborn baby.

They love their infant, want to protect their baby, and just hope that their child may have a safe and happy life.

UNICEF's activities provide hope to refugee parents: even though they live in a settlement, they may still be able to protect their newborn child.

EDUCATION

Ensuring access to formal education is a key priority for UNICEF. With approximately 500,000 refugee children of pre-school, primary, and secondary school age in Lebanon, UNICEF and other aid agencies, along with the Lebanese Ministry of Education, have developed education programmes aimed at meeting the development needs of both refugees and vulnerable Lebanese children. The programmes offer assistance with enrolment, transportation, school supplies and the teaching workforce. Of equal benefit is that all parents have been exempted from paying enrolment fees at public schools and the requirement for refugee children to present a valid residency permit on enrolment has been lifted.

Visitors can see the very real benefits of UNICEF's work just by spending time in the classroom. Here the children are safe and free just to learn, grow and develop.

The patience that the teachers exhibit is humbling. Equipped with the skills to teach children impacted by trauma, they display extraordinary compassion and understanding. Each child is encouraged to grow and develop – no matter how severe their individual disability.

Learning and the classroom take many different forms. Just like many children in wealthy countries, these young refugee girls display a love of music and dance. These lessons are a great way to learn and develop freedom of expression.

Sport is used to teach teamwork. The physical exercise also helps the children to expend energy and feel good.

Fun exercise games also teach coordination. In many respects, the principles and tools for learning and development are universal.

Primary school children often bear the weight and responsibility of caring for younger siblings.

This is not a place where parents drive to drop off and collect children from school. The choice to attend classes is often driven by the child's own motivation and commitment.

A 'Back to School' campaign has been used to raise awareness about the importance of education for all refugee children, and ways they can access it.

UNICEF works with the Lebanese Ministry of Education to run additional classes to meet the demand for education and to help overcome language problems. One challenge for the refugees is that English and French are also languages for learning in Lebanon, not just Arabic. These kids are bright, capable and hungry to learn.

They may be young and married, but they still deserve an education. For themselves and for their children, child brides need to be encouraged to continue their education and be supported as they learn to juggle the demands of school and family life.

Without education, what hope do these children have?

Without education, how can this boy conceive of a different life?

FATIMA

The Hand of Fatima (or Hamsa) is rich with many meanings; it is a symbol of patience, blessings, power and strength against difficulties. Common traditionally in North African Arabic and Berber cultures, for centuries Fatima's Hand has been regarded as a powerful talisman for good luck and for protection, a symbol of resilience in the face of adversity, whether affixed to the front door of a home, or worn as an amulet on the body. It is a motif that has now found its way into popular western culture.

Until we visited the Bekaa Valley, some of us knew about the Hand of Fatima, but we had no personal connection to it. Then we sat with a woman named Fatima and we watched her hold her 3-year-old daughter Faten in her hands. We saw her physically protect her child, as her eyes spoke of the hardship she had endured and her voice spoke of her fear for her daughter's future. Seeing her hands cradle Faten, we realised that there, in Fatima's hands, sat hope. Never again would the Hand of Fatima merely be a motif for us; it had become our talisman for hope, for Fatima, her family, and their fellow refugees.

Spending time in the refugee settlements enables you to see a person and not a news flash. Sitting in their home, their classroom, and their meeting place lets you experience their humanity, laughter and generosity of spirit. Truly they are people just trying to make the best of a very difficult situation. They chose to save their lives, but they would love to just be able to go home to their country and to their old way of life.

Being in their presence makes you realise that the energy expended to survive has stripped them of any guise. They are beyond pretence – they simply present you with themselves and in their eyes they show you their hopes and fears, sadness and blessings, strength and humility.

Visiting the informal settlements we met many people and were fortunate to connect with some extraordinary souls, five of whom were named 'Fatima' and who shone with the light of courage and dignity. Perhaps they were named after the Holy Prophet Muhammad's daughter Fatima Zahra, "the shining one"? Perhaps not. Whoever their namesakes are, allow us to introduce them to you.

Hope is born in the soul, empowers the heart, and creates the strength to keep moving forward one step at a time. Without hope, the will to act can be lost; the desire to fight against the odds is eroded.

Fatima, mother of Asmahan and Faten, holds anguish in her eyes. She suffers with her desire to protect and her limited ability to offer hope to her daughters. She asks simply not to be forgotten.

Fatima, mother of Wardeh, sits stoically in silence. She listens and observes. She hopes to protect her daughter from early marriage. She is proud and present in her bearing as she gifts an image of herself.

Fatima, mother of Mohammad, shines with love for her son. She exudes a purity and grace that defies the road of rubble that she sits on and the flimsy tent she now calls home.

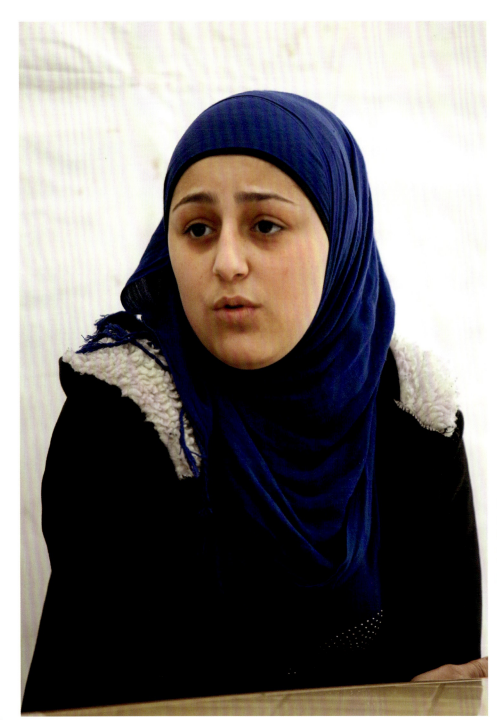

Fatima, child bride, is fifteen years old. She attends life-lesson classes, but her eyes speak of lessons that a child should never have had to learn. Within her air of sadness glimmers a light of hope.

Fatima, her father's "little angel" and sister of Ahmar, is twelve years old. She watched her best friend die after a market bomb. She survived and escaped the city of Homs, but often sits alone and cries, sad for her lost friend. She has watched a neighbour of a similar age recently marry, but does not think her father will propose it for her, nor that her family will support it.

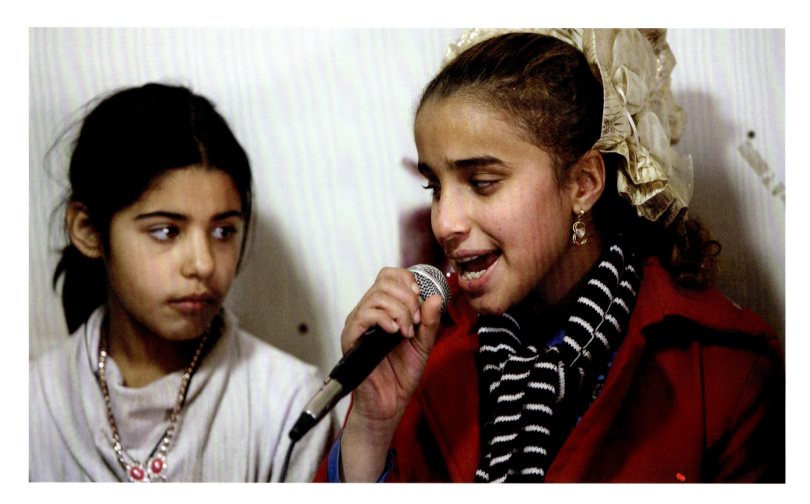

Hope is an innate belief that charges us to use our life force to create change and deliver our dreams. It is the energy that helps us to be happy in the moment and holds us strong when our body tires and spirit flags. It is what gives us compassion to help our friends.

Our lives may not be perfect, we may be exhausted, fearful, saddened, lonely and depressed, but if we have hope we hold a candle that sheds light. Even a flickering candle holds light; all we have to do is protect it while it strengthens. With unity, the light of hope burns stronger.

These women sit together and support each other. They celebrate each other's joys – such as pride in a daughter's ability to count to ten in English – and understand the strength that comes from both asking for and offering to help.

How strange it is that those who have so little are rarely limited in their generosity. The women's meeting place may have been on the side of the road, but their civility and ceremony in offering of a drink of coffee held a nobility of gesture more befitting a fine hotel. These women humbled us with their willingness to share their souls, their hopes and their sustenance. How could we ever forget them!

REFLECTION

There are many special moments that will be remembered from UNICEF NZ's visit to the Bekaa Valley. Each person in the delegation will treasure their own particular highlight, the moment that touched their heart.

Sonny Bill Williams told Mike McRoberts that he had initially been motivated to visit the Syrian refugee settlements for selfish reasons – he had thought that the journey and understanding the refugees' plight might help him be a better person. The reality is that having spent time with the refugees, visited a home, played sports with children, spoken directly with youth and at-risk girls, and observed the classes and activities in the UNICEF and Beyond Borders child-safe spaces, we each came away with a life-changing experience that has grown our compassion and understanding of this unique crisis.

In young Fatima, we met an extraordinary girl. She told us that she would like to be a singer when she grows up; with her courage and determination she might just make her dream come true. With teenage Mohammad we learnt that it is not the possessions that they had in Syria that the older children miss, but rather the education and the chance to earn a decent living.

The young pre-school children showed us that they are just like children the world over, needing love, a safe space, and people who care to help them grow and develop. Finally, it was fourteen-year-old Ahmar who humbled us with his courage and sense of responsibility. He exemplified the strength and resilience of the young men who work in landowners' fields or take menial manual labour jobs to shoulder the financial responsibilities to provide for their parents and siblings.

From each of the children we learnt that their hope for the future rests on their ability to be healthy and protected and to get an education – all that UNICEF works towards.

Reflecting on the informal settlements during his TV3 interview, Sonny Bill said he was particularly struck by the fact that the refugees wanted to be doing something – they wanted to be helping themselves, working, providing for their families – and yet they were able to do nothing. It was that enforced helplessness which moved him to say:

"Something has gone drastically wrong in the world today…I'm not a politician and all of that stuff is unknown to me… but what I do know is people should not be living like this.
These people are just like us and it's a sad world we are living in at the moment."

These are extraordinary children, living challenging and difficult lives, and somehow in the midst of loss and displacement they are choosing to cherish hope. In the children's own words: "Hope is my weapon". With UNICEF's support they have a chance to be able to grow strong, find the courage to wield the light of hope, and to create a positive future for themselves.

How could we choose not to help them?

Hope is my Weapon...!

ACKNOWLEDGEMENTS

All the author's royalties and net proceeds from this book will be donated by Beatnik Publishing to UNICEF NZ for the Syrian Refugee programmes in Lebanon.

In addition, the author gratefully wishes to ackowledge the considerable commitment and generosity of the following people, without whom the creation of this book would not have been possible:
B Godfrey, J & C de Lapuente, H Saad, J Scanlon, and the Teo Family.

She also wishes to thank the following people for their kind support and contribution:
G Biggar, C Eid, M Greatbatch, E & S Mahon, G Morris, K Rittson-Thomas, H Scotts, K & A Spring, and C & H Varney.

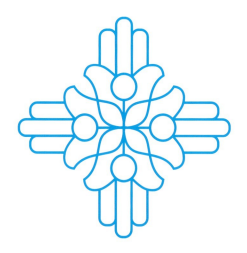